Fun and Games

Fife Council Education Department
King's Road Primary School
King's Crescent, Rosyth KY11 2RS

Compiled by Wendy Body

Acknowledgements

We are grateful to the following for permission to reproduce copyright material: the author's agent for the story 'Cup Final For Charlie' from *Cup Final For Charlie* by Joy Allen Copyright © 1981 Joy Allen (1st pub. Hamish Hamilton, 1981); Escargot Productions Limited for the story 'Chilly Billy' from *Amazing Adventures of Chilly Billy* by Peter Mayle © Escargot Productions Limited 1980; William Heinemann Limited for the story 'Mr Kendal thinks he has a Good Idea' from *The Lily Pickle Band Book* by Gwen Grant; Ward Lock Educational Co. Limited for the story 'Return To Air' by Philippa Pearce from *Tales 3* compiled by Geoffrey Summerfield.

We are grateful to the following for permission to reproduce photographs and badges: Arsenal Football Club, page 46 below left; Aston Villa Football Club, page 46 above right; All Sport, pages 18, 19 below left, 20, 46 above left 46 below left; Camera Press, pages 19 above left (photo: John Evans), 19 above right (photo: Colman Doyle), 19 below right (photo: John Evans); Celtic Football Club, page 47 below left; Colorsport, pages 47 above left and below right; Everton Football Club, page 47 above left; Liverpool Football Club, page 46 below right; Manchester United Football Club, page 46 above left; Rangers Football Club, page 47 above right; Tottenham Hotspur Football Club, page 47 below right.

Pages 16-19, 20-1 and 46-7 were written by Bill Boyle and Debbie Fox. We are grateful to K. S. Duncan at the British Olympic Association for assistance.

Illustrators include: David Woodward pp. 4-15; Peter Kesteven pp.: 16-18; Paul Collicutt þp. 20-1, 63-4, David Wong pp. 22-31; Peter Foster pp. 32-3; Michael Salter pp. 34-45; Maggie Ling and Jones Sewell and Associates pp. 46-7; Deborah Pollard pp. 48-62.

Contents

Chilly Billy

Every year, about the time when the owners of fridges
go off on their holidays, Chilly Billy and his friends held
The Great Annual Fridge Olympics and Frozen Sports.

Billy's friends came from far and wide, and no
wonder; this was the most important event of the frozen
sporting year.

Because there were so many visitors, Billy couldn't
possibly fit them all into his home behind the ice cube
tray. So they had to sleep packed head-to-toe like
sardines in those narrow shelves inside the door.

And what a grand time they had. Every evening, there
was a party in the butter compartment, hide-and-seek
among the vegetables, and a remarkable game of
musical eggs, which I'll tell you about another time.

The days were spent training, and if you happened to be taking a stroll through the fridge, you had to keep your eyes open so as not to be bumped into by all the little men who would suddenly come whizzing round corners or leaping from an overhead shelf.

The events that made up the Fridge Olympics included just about every frozen sport you could think of, and a few unfrozen ones too.

The ski-runs were in the freezer compartment, and a ski-jump had been made by coating the sloping top of a milk carton with ice. After coming off the carton at great speed, the skiers, their tiny arms and legs whirling to help them go further, would land safely on a large and very squishy slice of lemon meringue pie. (Difficult to climb out of, just in case you ever think of jumping in it yourself.)

Then there were the acrobatics — swinging, twirling, and flying through the air from the shelf bars. Only the most daring and athletic were allowed to enter, because it was really quite dangerous.

And the biggest and strongest competitors had an event all to themselves: Tossing the Carrot.

The idea was to get hold of a carrot at the big end, balance it upright in the hands, and fling it as far as possible with a mighty heave. When you think that an ordinary size carrot of the kind you would eat weighs much more than any little man, you can understand what great strength is needed. (A good aim is needed as well. There are many sad stories of spectators being injured by badly tossed carrots.)

All these events, and many others, were included in the Fridge Olympics.

But the most important event of all, where the winner
won a huge gold medal, was the Great Cross-Refrigerator
Race. And that's what Chilly Billy had been training
for all year long.

Billy was very good at this race, and he hoped to win.
But he had a serious rival, a real expert at cross-
refrigerator racing who had come all the way from
Birmingham, where he lived and trained in a refrigerator
factory.

Nobody knew his real name; he was called the Mad
Jumper, because of his rolling eyes and amazing leaps,
and he was *huge*. He must have been nearly three
quarters of an inch tall, even without his boots on. And
that, for a tiny man, is very, very big.

For the last two days, the Mad Jumper hadn't joined in any of the games with the others. He'd just sat on his own, polishing his boots and glaring at Chilly Billy. He was determined to win, and he didn't intend to let Billy stop him.

At last, the day of the great race came. Bright and early, all the spectators settled down along the race course, which started at the bottom left-hand corner of the fridge, and ended at the top right-hand corner.

A roar went up from the crowd as Chilly Billy and the Mad Jumper took their places at the starting line. Billy, who isn't very big at the best of times, looked even smaller next to the giant Jumper. But he wasn't going to let that worry him.

I may be small, he thought to himself, but I'm as nippy as they come. Big as he is, I'll keep up with him.

They were ready.

Billy's friend Lily, who was starting the race, called out, "On your marks."

Billy and the Mad Jumper shuffled their boots and flexed their toes nervously.

"Right," said Lily, "when I pop this Rice Krispie, that's the signal to be off. The first one to reach the top gets the gold medal and a kiss from me."

"Save your breath," said the Mad Jumper with a nasty laugh. "I'll want a *big* kiss when I win."

9

Billy was furious, but before he could say anything Lily popped the starting Krispie and the race was on.

The two racers had completely different styles. Billy was running as fast as he could along the bottom of the fridge, but the Mad Jumper looked more like a kangaroo. He was taking huge hops, and it wasn't long before he was out in front.

He looked back at Billy and sneered. "What's the matter, shorty? Have you got lead in your boots?" And he hopped away, laughing his nasty laugh.

Billy saved his breath, for they were just coming up to the first wall, and he was going to need all his energy to climb up it.

Even the Mad Jumper couldn't hop up walls, so by the time they had climbed to the first shelf, Billy had caught up and they were side by side as they came to the first swing of the race.

They had to swing across the shelf to reach the opposite wall, and this is where Billy's training started to pay off.

He was like a flying monkey, swinging round and round on one bar and then whizzing off to catch another bar further on. And when they reached the far wall, Billy was well ahead.

By now, the spectators were all jumping up and down with excitement. They didn't like the Mad Jumper's nasty ways, and they wanted Billy to beat him. But the race wasn't over yet, by a long way.

The shelf that the two had reached was a solid one, and the Jumper was catching up on Billy by leaps and bounds and hops.

They were neck and neck. Now the Jumper had overtaken Billy, and was getting further ahead with each hop.

Suddenly, hidden from the crowd by an icicle, the
Jumper stopped, took something out of his pocket, and
squirted it all over the shelf before hopping off again.

Billy was running so fast that he couldn't stop to see
what the Jumper had squirted on the floor. And then, to
his horror, he found out what it was. His sucker boots
started slipping and sliding until he could hardly stand,
let alone run. That wicked Jumper had covered the floor
with cooking oil so that Billy's suckers couldn't suck!
And there was another wall to climb before the final
stretch of the race.

What was Billy to do?

Slipping and sliding and trying to run, Billy thought the hardest he'd ever thought in his life.

Then, just as he reached the wall where his sucker boots would be useless, he had a brainwave.

Unwinding his long woolly scarf, he threw it up and over the bars of the shelf above him so that it made a kind of rope. Kicking off his slippery boots, he climbed up his scarf and on to the next shelf.

The Jumper, meanwhile, was hopping along quite slowly with his hands in his pockets, feeling quite sure that he had put Billy out of the race for good.

So when the cheers of the crowd behind him made him turn around, he could hardly believe his eyes. Chilly Billy had given himself a push off from the wall, and was sliding along the shelf at headlong speed on his socks.

The Jumper hopped and bounded and jumped his

hardest, but it was no good. Billy slid past him like a rocket, his trusty scarf streaming behind him, and crossed the finishing line so fast that he crashed into the cheering spectators before he could stop.

"Oh Billy," said Lily, giving him his gold medal and a big kiss. "Well done! I'm so proud of you."

"Phew," puffed Billy, "if it wasn't for those socks you knitted for me, I'd never have won. They must be the fastest socks in the world."

And that was how Chilly Billy won the Great Cross-Refrigerator Race, much to everyone's delight.

As for the Mad Jumper, he was sent back to Birmingham in disgrace, and forbidden by the Fridge Olympic Committee to enter any more races until he stopped his nasty tricks.

And the gold medal is still hanging up on the wall of Billy's bedroom today, next to his world-beating socks.

Written by Peter Mayle,
illustrated by Dand Wood Ward

THE OLYMPIC GAMES

The Olympic Games began in ancient Greece
and were one of many religious games and festivals.
The first recorded date of the Games taking place was 776 BC
and they were held every four years at Olympia.

There was only one race in the first Olympic Games. This was called the *stade* and it was about 192 metres long. At this time, only men could enter the Games. In fact, any married women who wanted to attend were threatened with being thrown off a nearby cliff. Winners of the race received crowns of wild olive leaves.

More and more events were introduced as the years went by. One of the most popular events was chariot racing.

By the fourth century the Games had lost their reputation. In AD 393,
the first Christian Emperor of Rome banned the Games.

In 1894, the Frenchman Baron de Coubertin set up the modern
International Olympic Committee. The first modern Olympic Games
were held in Athens in 1896.

In 1908 a standard, or common, gold medal was adopted. Since 1928 the front of the medal has had the same design for each Olympic Games; the back of the medal has had a different design for each Games.

Olympic Records

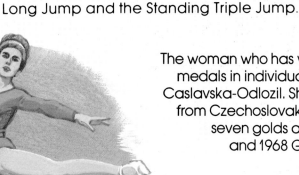

The man who has won the most gold medals in individual events is Ray Ewry of the United States of America. He won ten golds between 1900-1908 – for the Standing High Jump, the Standing Long Jump and the Standing Triple Jump.

The woman who has won the most gold medals in individual events is Vera Caslavska-Odlozil. She was a gymnast from Czechoslovakia and she won seven golds at the 1964 and 1968 Games.

The most gold medals won by one person in an Olympic Games is seven. Mark Spitz, the American swimmer, won four golds for individual races and three for relay events in the summer of 1972.

The most gold medals won in individual events at one Games is five by speed skater Eric Heiden, an American, at Lake Placid, USA, in 1980.

The youngest person to win an Olympic Gold was a French boy who coxed the winning Dutch rowing pair in 1900. His name is not known (as he was a substitute at the last minute), but he was not older than ten, and he could have been as young as seven.

The oldest competitor in the Games was Oscar Swahn of Sweden, who, at the age of 72 years and 280 days, won a silver medal for shooting. This was in 1920.

An outstanding single performance in Olympic history was Bob Beamon's long jump of 8.90 metres at the 1968 Games in Mexico City. This leap added 55 centimetres to the previous world record.

Nadia Comaneci from Romania was the first gymnast to score a maximum 10 points. She was 14 years old. She achieved this perfect score six more times at the same Games in 1976.

Los Angeles-1984

At the 1984 Los Angeles Olympics, Tessa Sanderson became the first British woman to win a javelin gold medal. Her fellow British athlete, Fatima Whitbread, took the bronze medal in the event.

Zola Budd caused a sensation at the 1984 Olympics by running in the women's 1500 metres in her bare feet.

Carl Lewis was an American hero in the Los Angeles Olympics. He won three individual gold medals and one relay gold.

Sebastian Coe set a new Olympic record for the 1500 metres in these Games.

Daley Thompson
SUPERSTAR!

Daley Thompson has won the World, Olympic and Commonwealth decathlon championships. The decathlon is regarded as the supreme test of stamina and performance, because over a two-day period the athletes must compete in ten separate field and track events.

Event 1
The 100 metres

Event 2
The long jump

Event 3
The shot put

Event 10
The 1500 metres

Event 4
The high jump

Event 9
The javelin

Event 5
The 400 metres

Event 8
The pole vault

Event 7
The discus

Event 6
The 110 metres hurdles

20

Daley Thompson – OLYMPIC HERO

Daley was born in Notting Hill, London, in 1958.

His headmaster took Daley to the local Haywards Heath Harriers athletics club, where Daley soon became an outstanding sprinter.

At the age of 16, Daley won his first decathlon competition. Later that year, Daley broke the British Junior decathlon record by scoring 7,100 points.

When he was 17, Daley made the British team for the 1976 Montreal Olympic Games. At his first attempt, he finished in eighteenth place.

In May 1980, Daley broke the world decathlon record at Gotzis, Austria, with a massive total of 8,622 points.

In July of the same year, in the Lenin Stadium, Moscow, Daley won his first Olympic Gold – a lifetime ambition.

In 1983, Daley was awarded the Membership of the British Empire (MBE). He received his medal from the Queen at Buckingham Palace.

Daley won his second Gold at the 1984 Los Angeles Olympics.

RETURN TO AIR

The Ponds are very big, so that at one end people bathe and at the other end they fish. Old chaps with bald heads sit on folding stools and fish with rods and lines, and little kids squeeze through the railings and wade out into the water to fish with nets. But the water's much deeper at our end of the Ponds, and that's where we bathe. You're not allowed to bathe there unless you can swim; but I've always been able to swim. They used to say that was because fat floats—well, I don't mind. They call me Sausage.

Only, I don't dive—not from any diving-board, thank you. I have to take my glasses off to go into the water, and I can't see without them, and I'm just not going to dive, even from the lowest diving-board, and that's that, and they stopped nagging about it long ago.

Then, this summer, they were all on to me to learn duck-diving. You're swimming on the surface of the water and suddenly you up-end yourself just like a duck and dive down deep into the water, and perhaps you swim about a bit underwater, and then come up again. I daresay ducks begin doing it soon after they're born. It's different for them.

So I was learning to duck-dive — to swim down to the bottom of the Ponds, and pick up a brick they'd thrown in, and bring it up again. You practise that in case you have to rescue anyone from drowning — say, they'd sunk for the third time and gone to the bottom. Of course, they'd be bigger and heavier than a brick, but I suppose you have to begin with bricks and work up gradually to people.

The swimming-instructor said, "Sausage, I'm going to throw the brick in —" It was a brick with a bit of old white flannel round it, to make it show up underwater. "— Sausage, I'm going to throw it in, and you go *after* it — go *after* it, Sausage, and get it before it reaches the bottom and settles in the mud, or you'll never get it."

He'd made everyone come out of the water to give me a chance, and they were standing watching. I could see them blurred along the bank, and I could hear them talking and laughing.

But there wasn't a sound in the water except me just treading water very gently, waiting. And then I saw the brick go over my head as the instructor threw it, and there was a splash as it went into the water ahead of me; and I thought: I can't do it—my legs won't up-end this time—they feel just flabby—they'll float, but they won't up-end—they *can't* up-end—it's different for ducks…But while I was thinking all that, I'd taken a deep breath, and then my head really went down and my legs went up into the air—I could feel them there, just air around them, and then there was water round them, because I was going down into the water, after all. Right down into the water; straight down…

At first my eyes were shut, although I didn't know I'd shut them. When I did realise, I forced my eyelids up against the water to see. Because, although I can't see much without my glasses, as I've said, I don't believe anyone could see much underwater in those Ponds; so I could see as much as anyone.

The water was like
a thick greeny-brown
lemonade, with wispy little
things moving very slowly about in it
—or perhaps they were just movements of
the water, not things at all; I couldn't tell. The brick
had a few seconds' start on me, of course, but I could still
see a whitish glimmer that must be the flannel round it: it
was ahead of me, fading away into the lower water, as I
moved after it.

The funny thing about swimming underwater is its being
so still and quiet and shady down there, after all the air and
sunlight and splashing and shouting just up above. I was
shut right in by the quiet, greeny-brown water, just me
alone with the brick ahead of me, both of us making
towards the bottom.

The Ponds are deep, but I knew they weren't too deep;
and, of course, I knew I'd enough air in my lungs from the
breath I'd taken. I knew all that.

Down we went, and the lemonade-look quite went from the water, and it became just a dark blackish-brown, and you'd wonder you could see anything at all. Especially as the bit of white flannel seemed to have come off the brick by the time it reached the bottom and I'd caught up with it. The brick looked different down there, anyway, and it had already settled right into the mud—there was only one corner left sticking up. I dug into the mud with my fingers and got hold of the thing, and then I didn't think of anything except getting up again with it into the air.

Touching the bottom like that had stirred up the mud, so that I began going up through a thick cloud of it. I let myself go up—they say fat floats you know—but I was shooting myself upwards, too. I was in a hurry.

The funny thing was, I only began to be afraid when I was going back. I suddenly thought: perhaps I've swum underwater much too far—perhaps I'll come up at the far end of the Ponds among all the fishermen and foul their lines and perhaps get a fish-hook caught in the flesh of my cheek. And all the time I was going up quite quickly, and the water was changing from brown-black to green-brown and then to bright lemonade. I could almost see the sun shining through the water, I was so near the surface. It wasn't until then that I felt really frightened: I thought I was moving much too slowly and I'd never reach the air again in time.

Never the air again...

Then suddenly I was at the surface—I'd exploded back from the water into the air. For a while I couldn't think of anything, and I couldn't do anything except let out the old breath I'd been holding and take a couple of fresh, quick ones and tread water—and hang on to that brick. Pond water was trickling down inside my nose and into my mouth, which I hate. But there was air all round and above, for me to breathe, to live.

And then I noticed they were shouting from the bank. They were cheering and shouting, "Sausage! Sausage!" and the instructor was hallooing with his hands round his mouth, and bellowing to me: "What on earth have you got there, Sausage?"

So then I turned myself properly round—I'd come up almost facing the fishermen at the other end of the Pond, but otherwise only a few feet from where I'd gone down; so that was all right. I turned round and swam to the bank and they hauled me out and gave me my glasses to have a look at what I'd brought up from the bottom. Because it wasn't a brick. It was just about the size and shape of one, but it was a tin—an old, old tin box with no paint left on it and all brown-black slime from the bottom of the Ponds. It was as heavy as a brick because it was full of mud. Don't get excited, as we did: there was nothing there but mud. We strained all the mud through our fingers, but there wasn't anything else there—not even a bit of old sandwich or the remains of bait. I thought there might have been, because the tin could have belonged to one of the old chaps that have always fished at the other end of the Ponds.

They often bring their dinners with them in bags or tins, and they have tins for bait, too. It could have been dropped into the water at their end of the Ponds and got moved to our end with the movement of the water. Otherwise I don't know how that tin box can have got there. Anyway, it must have been there for years and years, by the look of it. When you think, it might have stayed there for years and years longer; perhaps stayed sunk underwater for ever.

I've cleaned the tin up and I keep it on the mantelpiece at home with my coin collection in it. I had to duck-dive later for another brick, and I got it all right, without being frightened at all; but it didn't seem to matter as much as coming up with the tin. I shall keep the tin as long as I live, and I might easily live to be a hundred.

Philippa Pearce
Illustrated by *David Wong*

33

CUP FINAL FOR CHARLIE

Charlie's Uncle Tim has two tickets for the Cup Final — one for himself and one for Charlie . . .

Charlie's news caused quite a stir at school.

"Lucky thing," Joe said. "You can borrow my Arsenal scarf."

"You can wear my Arsenal hat too, if you like," offered Bill Wykes. "That is, if you're not too big headed!"

"Watch it!" warned Charlie putting up his fists and laughing. Bill dodged behind Joe for protection.

In break-time they all made Charlie a banner to wave. Joe borrowed some poster paint when Mrs Eve wasn't looking and painted ARSENAL FOR EVER. The EVER part ran down to the bottom of the banner.

Charlie held it as high as he could. "It's super. I can't wait for Saturday. I only wish you could all come with me."

Saturday came at last. Charlie sat by the window waiting for Uncle Tim.

"Here he is!" Charlie shouted.

He rammed Bill's red and white Arsenal bobble-cap on his head and wrapped Joe's scarf around his neck.

"Wow! You look great!" Uncle Tim said as Charlie bounded into the kitchen. "All you need now is this red and white rosette." He pinned it carefully on to Charlie's shirt.

"This scarf is throttling me!" Charlie was really hot.

"You'll be boiled," Mike said. "Wish I was coming."

Uncle Tim sympathised, "I'll try and get you a ticket next time. As it's nearly Charlie's birthday, I thought it could be his treat."

"Anyway, you're Captain of the football game here," Charlie said. "They couldn't do without us both."

As Uncle Tim and Charlie were driving away they heard a great shout.

"STOP! STOP!" Dad yelled. They turned round to see Mum and Dad running towards the car with Charlie's banner between them.

"Thanks," Charlie gasped as they passed it through the window. "Fancy me forgetting this. All my mates are watching out for the banner on the television this afternoon."

The coach was waiting for them in the car-park of "The King's Arms". Uncle Tim drew up with a screech of brakes and everyone cheered as they clambered aboard.

"You sit at the back with the other kids," Uncle Tim said. "You can wave your banner and enjoy yourself."

There were seven other boys and girls all crammed on to the long back seat. They wore an assortment of red and white shirts, socks, scarves and hats.

"Shove up, Tony," a red-faced boy called Mac shouted.

"What's your name?" another boy asked.

"Charlie."

"O.K. Charlie. Here. Catch! Have a packet of crisps."

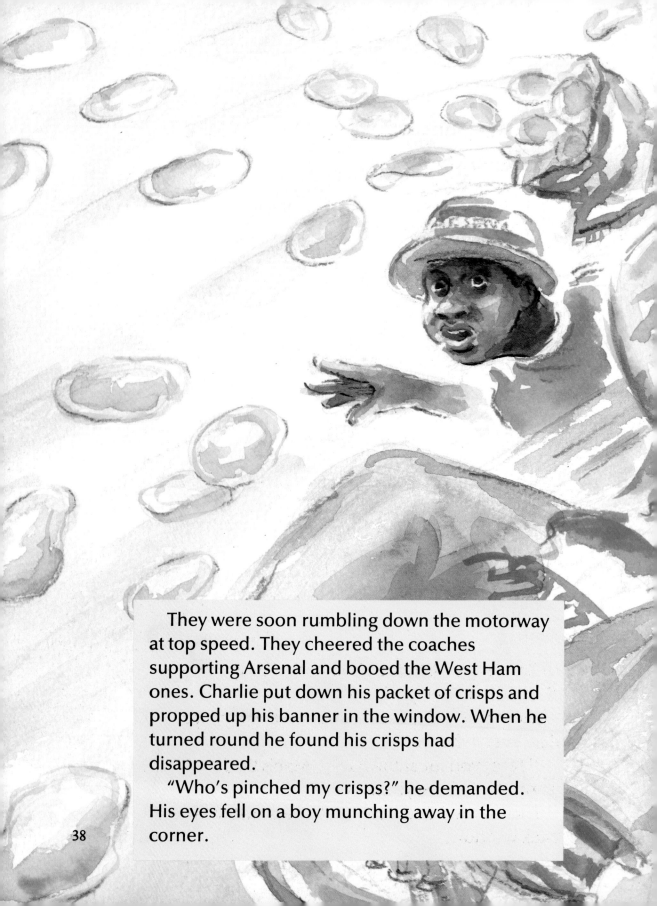

They were soon rumbling down the motorway at top speed. They cheered the coaches supporting Arsenal and booed the West Ham ones. Charlie put down his packet of crisps and propped up his banner in the window. When he turned round he found his crisps had disappeared.

"Who's pinched my crisps?" he demanded. His eyes fell on a boy munching away in the corner.

"Jason, give Charlie his crisps," Tony shouted. "You've had one packet already."

Jason threw the packet at Charlie and crisps flew everywhere.

"Here, you lot at the back," Mac's Dad warned. "Behave yourselves."

They settled down to watch the traffic from the back window.

39

"A West Ham supporters' coach is behind us," yelled Tony. "The driver is waving his fist."

"Hey up!" Mac shouted, "he's drawing out to overtake us."

"Faster. FASTER!" they all screamed at Stevie the driver. "Don't let West Ham get by us."

Stevie put his foot hard down and suddenly there was a loud explosion followed by an even louder choking sound.

Stevie pulled into the side. Luckily a few yards further on there was a service station and he managed to persuade a mechanic from the garage to look at the engine. Charlie leant against the window to watch him at work.

"Will we be in time for the kick-off?" Charlie whispered anxiously to Uncle Tim.

"Hope so, with a bit of luck," he replied. "We might not have much time for our picnic though."

"Let's have it while the engine is being mended," suggested Mac's Dad. They all helped to carry the picnic from the boot into the coach.

"Super!" Charlie gasped. "I've never seen a picnic like this before."

"There are chicken legs, sausages on sticks and scotch eggs," Mac's Dad said.

"Coke for the kids and beer for the mums and dads," Uncle Tim added. They all tucked in. By the time they had finished, the coach was mended and they were rattling along again at top speed.

Charlie was jammed in on all sides. "Bit of a squash," he shouted to Uncle Tim. There was a brass band playing on the pitch, their instruments flashing in the bright sun. It was wonderful! When the players ran on Charlie screamed and yelled. Tony held one stick of the banner and Charlie the other; they waved it frantically.

At last the game began and Charlie had never seen football like it.

The boy in front of them had brought a bucket to stand on. The bucket was white, with blue and claret stripes on it.

"What a good idea," Charlie remarked.

"Stop wobbling about on that bucket, George," a thin, long-faced man snapped.

"He's a West Ham supporter," Tony replied scathingly. "Give him a shove so that he falls off!"

Just at this moment, West Ham United scored a goal, and George was so excited that he fell off his bucket without being pushed.

At half-time West Ham were still in the lead and the singing and cheering never stopped.

"Hold the banner as high as you can so that all my school-mates can see it," Charlie shouted at Tony.

"ARSENAL! ARSENAL!" they screamed in unison.

In the second half, Arsenal tried as hard as they could to score a goal but they never quite managed it. As the final whistle blew, Charlie's heart sank.

"Never mind," Uncle Tim said, "the most important thing is to learn how to be a good loser. We can't always win."

"And it was a great game," added Charlie.

Written by Joy Allen,
illustrated by Michael Salter

Name of club:

Manchester United

Nickname: Red Devils

Stadium: Old Trafford

Colours: Red and white with black trim

Things to know:

Manchester United became the first English team to win the European Cup. This was in 1968.

Bobby Charlton holds the English International goal-scoring record with 49 goals. His first goal was in 1958 and his last was in 1970.

Bobby Charlton

Name of club:

Aston Villa

Nickname: The Villans

Stadium: Villa Park

Colours: Claret and blue

Things to know:

Aston Villa were one of the twelve clubs who joined the first football league a hundred years ago. They were runners-up in the very first league season (1888–9).

Villa brought the European Cup to the Midlands by beating Bayern Munich in the 1982 Cup Final.

Name of club:

Arsenal

Nickname: The Gunners

Stadium: Highbury

Colours: Red and white

Things to know:

In the 1930s Arsenal won the League Championships five times.

Arsenal have won the FA Cup five times at Wembley Stadium.

Name of club:

Liverpool

Nickname: The Reds *or* The Pool

Stadium: Anfield

Colours: Red and white

Things to know:

Liverpool have won the European Cup four times, which is more than any other British team.

The team went from the Second Division to the First Division championships when their manager was Bill Shankly.

"Which is your favourite team?"

Name of club: Everton

Nickname: The Toffees

Stadium: Goodison Park

Colours: Royal blue and white

Things to know:

Dixie Dean was an Everton player who was famous for scoring a lot of goals with his head.

In 1985 Everton won their first European trophy beating Rapide Vienna in the Cup Winners Cup Final by three goals to one.

Dixie Dean

Name of club: Rangers

Nickname: The Gers

Stadium: Ibrox

Colours: Red, white and blue

Things to know:

In 1972 Rangers won their first European trophy by beating Dynamo Moscow in the Cup Winners Cup Final.

Rangers have won the Scottish League Championships 36 times — between 1899 and 1978.

SCOTTISH Premier

		Home					Away					
	P	W	D	L	F	A	W	D	L	F	A	Pts
Rangers	44	18	2	2	45	6	13	5	4	40	17	69
Celtic	44	16	5	1	57	17						

Name of club: Celtic

Nickname: The Bhoys

Stadium: Celtic Park

Colours: Green and white hoops

Things to know:

Celtic were the first British side to win the European Cup. This was in 1967.

Jock Stein was the manager during many of their triumphs. He later became manager of the Scotland team.

Name of club: Tottenham Hotspur

Nickname: Spurs

Stadium: White Hart Lane

Colours: White and navy

Things to know:

Tottenham have won the Cup Winners Cup once (1963) and the UEFA Cup twice (1972 and 1984). UEFA stands for Union of European Football Associations.

In the 1960–61 season the captain, Danny Blanchflower, led Spurs to the first "double" this century. They won both the League Championship and the FA Cup.

Danny Blanchflower

Mr Kendal ~~has~~ *thinks he* has a Good Idea

I am writing this story under a false name as I do not want anyone to know it is me that has written it.

In some countries, when they find a dead body, unless it has its name written on the soles of its feet or in blue ink on its arm—and that doesn't happen very often, I can tell you—they call these bodies John Doe or Jane Doe, depending on whether it's a lass or a lad, you know.

Well, I am going to sign this "Jane Doe" because, if I do not, then I shall be as dead as any dead body myself when certain people have read it.

The most certain person of all would be Mavis Jarvis, who is about twelve feet tall, twelve feet wide and a hundred feet thick in the head. You could spit rivets at her head and she wouldn't even notice them going in, she's that thick.

E. Harris says Mavis J. was made out of a Do-It-Yourself kit from Mackies Ironmongers.

"She don't feel rivets going in," he says, "because her head's full of 'em already."

I don't know about that. I'm willing to believe it though. All I do know is that they reckon when she was a baby, people used to look in her pram, go crosseyed and hand her a banana.

Well, I am halfway between twelve and thirteen years old. My Gran says she is halfway to heaven but she is very old with white hair and knows a lot.

I have got one Gran and one Mam and no Dad to speak of. The reason we don't speak of him is because he came into the kitchen one night when I was six years old and said to my Mam, "This is the end. I am going to seek my fortune." And he went to work at the dog food factory which closed down two weeks later.

My Mam said it was the factory's own fault for taking my Dad on.

"Never could keep anything, he couldn't," she says, and then my Dad went away and nobody's heard from him since.

I says to my Gran, "What were my Dad like, Gran?" and she says, "I'm saying nothing. All I ask you to remember is that if I hadn't been there, you'd have been answering to Honolulu Baby by now."

"Honolulu Baby?" I says and my Gran nods her head and goes, "Your Mam and Dad went to the pictures a week before you was born and saw this lass wearing nothing but a blade of grass and a smile and she was called Honolulu Baby. Your Dad thought that was a very good name." And Gran snorted and said I wasn't to bring the subject up again if I didn't mind because, speaking for herself, she was certain sure said subject would turn up one day of his own accord.

Well, I reckon a Dad as could call a person Honolulu Baby when they live round here is more trouble than he's worth.

Where I live is a mining town right on the far north tip of Nottinghamshire and if you tell people you live here, they go, "Oh yes. Stagecoach still running there, is it?" and think they are very funny which they are not.

This story I'm writing though is about our band. I thought I'd better write down about our band before I forget.

Mavis Jarvis had a part in the school play last Christmas as the front end of the horse carrying Prince Charming with his plastic shoe to old Cinderella there in the kitchen. She forgot to put the horse's head on when she went on the stage but it didn't make any difference. Two little kids at the front still gave her a carrot each.

Anyway, as I was saying. This story is really about our band which is called The Workton Whistler's Children's Jazz Band and Mr Kendal from Rat-Trap House, which is really the second block of flats where we all live, he's running it.

One day he gets all the kids and their Mams and Dads together and he says, "Now then, I want all them kids who 'asn't got nowt better to do to come to the Palace Gardens tonight." Then he sucks his breath in through his teeth till he whistles, wheee, he goes and looks at the Mams and Dads and says, "Band, you know," and winks with his left eye.

All the Mams and Dads say, "Right," and, "Yers, I should think so," and that's that.

Palace Gardens is a mucky great field with a scout hut on it, two goal posts and a river. Everybody goes there at night anyway.

So, this night, comes seven o'clock and there's Mr Kendal on the field and he's shouting, "Now come on, you lot. Let's get this show on the road," and we all look round for the show and find out that we're IT. We're the show.

It turns out then that Mr Kendal and Mrs Warren, from next door to us, they're going to make us into a band that plays and marches at the same time.

Mrs Warren says, "Don't you think that's a bit ambitious, Mr Kendal? Playing and marching at the same time?" But Mr Kendal shakes his head and says, "What! They don't know what they can do till they try," and tells us how, when he was in the army, he marched five days and five nights carrying his wounded pal.

I happen to know his wounded pal was an ant with a broken leg in a matchbox.

Mr Kendal told me so but he didn't tell any of the others.

I says to him, "How did you know it had got a broken leg, Mr Kendal?" because ants aren't very big so as you can have a look.

Mr Kendal tapped his nose with his finger and whispers, "It 'obbled when it walked."

I don't know what to think about that. None of the ants I've ever seen hobble but then, perhaps none of them had a broken leg.

Anyway, Mr Kendal gets us all together in the middle of the field and makes us stand in rows and E. Harris takes one look at this band and he says to Mr Kendal, "You ought to call it The Workton Wellies," which Mr Kendal didn't find very funny at all, but I looked round and there were eight of us in wellies and only thirteen in the band.

This band though is different from any other band I've ever heard about because you don't have to know how to play anything at all to be in it.

All you have to do to join is nod.

You nod when Mr Kendal says, "Who wants to play the kazoo?" You nod when he says, "And who wants to play the drums?" And you nod when he says, "And what about these here tambourines?"

Before you know where we are, there we are. A band. The Workton Whistler's Children's Jazz Band.

Mrs Warren shouts, "Now then. Who's going to be the girl who leads the band?" because even though there are lads in these bands, the leader always has to be a girl.

Before Mrs W. can draw another breath in order not to choke to death you know who's there, don't you, up at the front, pushing her nasty, piggy, little nose up against Mrs Warren's purple cardigan.

"Me," she says, and Mavis the Mandrake has struck again.

It says in the dictionary that mandrake is "a poisonous plant . . . thought to resemble human form and to shriek when plucked."

Well, that is very true of Mavis Jarvis, particularly the poisonous bit and she does only look a bit like a human being as well and you have to look hard to see even that. Unless, of course, they mean a monkey when they say "human form". Then you can see the likeness at a glance.

Anyway, there she is, going, "I'll lead the band. I'll lead the band."

"Why," says Mrs Warren. "It is nice to see you so keen, Mavis," and she looks round to see if anybody else wants to lead the band and there's Karen Green with her hand in the air.

"I'd like to lead the band as well," says Karen.

Mrs Warren goes, "Well," tut tut. "Two of you." And E. Harris says, "They're very quick these grownups, aren't they?" and Mr Kendal hears him and says, "Now then, don't let's have any of your cheek round here, my son."

So, Mrs Warren says, "Well, the thing is, girls, whoever leads the band has to be very good at tossing this stick up in the air and catching it and then tossing it up again. Not to mention twirling it round and round, all without dropping it and particularly without dropping it onto somebody's head."

Everybody thinks about this for a bit and I says to E. Harris, "What if you threw that stick up and it never came down again?" And E. Harris, he says, "Where is there for it to go in the sky?" And he looks up and goes on, "If you'd just look up, like I'm doing, you'd see the sky is empty."

"I know it's empty now," I says, "but what if God got fed up with people chucking their sticks in the air and he put his hand down and whipped one up to heaven?"

"Something like that happened when me and my rock group E. H. and the Dead Beats were practising in the school hall," E. Harris said. "Only it weren't the hand of God, it was the hand of the headmaster plucked our drumsticks out of thin air. Blinking hand like a rhubarb leaf, he had as well, and he wouldn't give us our sticks back no how. 'Terrible racket' he says, and puts them in his desk and there they are to this day."

E. Harris is in a band already. He has this rock group and they wear royal blue suits with black velvet collars and sequins round the cuffs, bootlace ties and a lot of scent. You can smell them a mile off and, if you try and stand near them, you keel over in a dead faint.

E. Harris says that is because they are the greatest, but it's really because they're the smelliest.

He asked me once if I'd go along and scream for them, so I did, and this bloke chucked them out because he said they were frightening all the little kids.

E. Harris wouldn't speak to me for about a month.

Then he says, "You were supposed to scream as if you liked us, not as if you'd just come face to face with Dracula."

I says to him, "Well, it weren't my fault. I was looking at you at the time."

Anyway, I thought I wouldn't put up my hand to lead the band in case the Hand of God came down and scooped me up instead.

Mavis Jarvis, though, she stuck her chest out and says, "I can do it, Mrs Warren. I can."

Then Karen Green, who can get very nasty when she wants to, she shoves old Mavis out of the way and goes, "And I can do it as well, Mrs Warren."

In the end Mrs Warren says, "Well, we shall just have to have a competition to decide, that's all." And she gives Mavis and Karen a stick each and tells them they've got half an hour to practise in.

"Go to the far side of the field out of harm's way," she says, "and in thirty minutes, we'll see who's best. Whoever's the best gets to lead the band," and she smiles. The only one who does. "I think that's fair, girls, isn't it?" she goes.

We're all going nudge nudge by now because although Mrs Warren thinks it's fair, we all know Mavis Jarvis.

Mr Kendal played war when he turned round and saw all his band vanishing over the field.

"Where you lot going?" he shouts, and somebody tells him we're going to watch Mavis Jarvis and Karen Green practising to be the leader of the band.

"Oh well," Mr Kendal says. "It was time for a break, anyhow." And he starts sorting out all his combs and bits of newspaper.

Trouble is, see, we haven't actually got any kazoos and things.

Mr Kendal says, "We'll just have to make do till we can afford some instruments. Them kazoos sound just like a comb and a bit of newspaper does, and we can use old tin plates for the cymbals." And then he stops and says, "We're going to have to raise some money, I can see that coming."

By the time we get to the corner of the field, Karen Green is beginning to look a bit pink because these sticks Mrs Warren's given them, they're like pit props.

Mavis J. was all right. She's built like a pit prop herself. She even looks like one. She was tossing her stick around as if it were a match.

Then she starts marching up and down like Mrs Warren showed her, throwing this stick in the air.

The first time she throws it up, she stands there grinning waiting for it to come down and E. Harris, me and Karen Green started running but this stick got us and it felled all of E. H., all of me, except for one foot, which was already on the ground anyway, and half of Karen Green. The other half of her was stood there yelling and screaming at Mavis J.

"Oops, sorry," says old M. and laughs her stupid head off.

Then Karen gets to have a go and she starts marching and we're all whistling 'The Grand Old Duke of York', except Mavis J. that is, she's sneering, and Karen just gets to where they're marching down again when she throws the stick as high as she can, catches it, twirls it round three times and then clumps Mavis Jarvis across the back of the legs with it.

Well, I must say that was the best part of the night. If every band night's going to be this good, I shan't miss one.

E. Harris, he takes one look at Karen Green and Mavis Jarvis with two pit props fighting it out between them and he says, "Well, I'm not going in no band with them telegraph poles in it, I can tell you that for nothing." But Mr Kendal, he says, "They're not supposed to knock folk to the ground." And he tells Mavis and Karen they'd better behave else they're out on their ears and then he turns round and says to me, "Here, you can lead the band."

Then he tells Karen and Mavis J. they'd better stop practising pretty darn quick while he's still got some band left, because everybody's on the ground holding their legs and arms and bits of their bodies and they're all moaning and groaning because of where these pit props have hit them.

Well, old Mavis doesn't like that at all and she throws her stick up and then marches off and leaves it to come down all on its own, which wasn't very clever, because it came down on top of old Mavis herself.

I thought E. Harris was having a heart attack because after one look at Mavis Jarvis flat on her back with this stick lying across her, he falls to the ground going erk, erk, erk. I had to bash him on the back to stop him choking. He didn't stop laughing for an hour.

He wasn't on his own, either. Three quarters of the band were down there with him.

Mr Kendal looks at them and then at Mavis and he says, "I can just see what kind of a band this is going to be." Then that lot who're Mavis Ug's pals, they go over and help her up and pick this stick up and next minute they're beating everybody around the head with it.

Mr Kendal and Mrs Warren say, "We're not having that," and they stop all the fighting, which was a shame as we were just getting going. Then Mr Kendal says, "Well, I think that's it for tonight and Lily Pickle here, she's the band leader."

That's my real name, Lily Pickle. Everybody calls me Piccalilli. They think they're so funny.

All I think is, what would have happened if I'd been called Honolulu Baby?

Written by Gwen Grant,
illustrated by Deborah Pollard

Words are *fun, too*

Glossary

ambition (*p. 21*)
to want success

assortment (*p. 37*)
collection of different
things or people

bait (*p. 30*)
food that is used for
catching fish or animals

bellowing (*p. 30*)
to make a loud, deep sound

clambered (*p. 37*)
to climb, not very easily

cox (*p. 18*)
a person who guides and
controls a rowing boat

in unison (*p. 44*)
together

kazoo (*p. 53*)
a toy musical instrument
that you blow into

keel over (*p. 56*)
to fall over sideways

piccalilli (*p. 62*)
spicy chopped
vegetables

pit props (*p. 59*)
pieces of wood that
support the roof of
a coal mine

pretty darn quick (*p. 61*)
very quickly

racket (*p. 55*)
a loud noise; also
used in sport (tennis)

Glossary continues on page 64

resemble *(p. 54)*
to look or be like

rivets *(p. 48)*
metal pins

runners-up *(p. 46)*
the team that comes
second

scooped *(p. 57)*
to take out or pick
up with the hands
or a spoon

sensation *(p. 19)*
excited interest

sequins *(p. 56)*
small circles of shining
plastic or metal,
used to decorate clothes

sneering *(p. 60)*
to look at a person as
if he or she is bad
or stupid

snorted *(p. 50)*
make a noise in the
nose to show you're
angry or amused

sprinter *(p. 21)*
fast runner

stadium *(p. 46)*
sports ground surrounded
by rows of seats for
spectators

stroll *(p. 5)*
a slow walk

substitute *(p. 18)*
a person or thing that
acts in the place of
another

sucker boots *(p. 12)*
boots that can cling
to a surface

supreme *(p. 20)*
highest; best

throttling *(p. 35)*
choking

treading water *(p. 26)*
keeping afloat in
water by moving your
legs up and down

wispy *(p. 27)*
thin; light; fluffy